How Charlie Feels

How Charlie Feels

Written by: Joy L.S. Hoffman & Danielle S. Kleist

Illustrated by: Matthew E. Howard

Tandem Light Press
950 Herrington Rd.
Suite C128
Lawrenceville, GA 30044

Tandem Light Press paperback edition

ISBN: 979-8-9882517-0-5
Library of Congress Control Number:

PRINTED IN THE UNITED STATES OF AMERICA

The Toddler
Book Series
is dedicated to
Hanna,
CJ, Emma,
& James.

Acknowledgments

Thank you to Tandem Light Press for believing in us and encouraging us to write stories about everyday children in everyday families. Thank you to our partners, John & Chris, for enthusiastically saying, "go for it!!" and not crushing our dreams. Special thanks to Hanna, CJ, Emma, & James, who inspire us every day to be better humans and parents.

-Danielle & Joy

CHARLIE

loves to play with toys and run

outside

with

FRIENDS.

It's hard for him to stop because he knows the fun will end.

Last night his

mommies

told him

that he had to come inside.

This made Charlie
REALLY SAD

so he fell down and cried.

The crying changed to **screaming** and his legs were kicking too.

This made his **mommies** **feel sad** and they didn't know what to do.

Charlie couldn't stop his **LEGS** from kicking here and there.

When mommy tried to help him, **HE GOT MAD** and pulled her hair.

Charlie feels

CONFUSED

when his body throws a fit.

He knows he's not supposed to

SCREAM

and

KICK or PULL or HIT.

But
sometimes
this is how he tells
his mommies that he's
sad.
And sometimes
it's the way he tells
his mommies that he's
mad.

Sometimes Charlie needs to

REST

or his tummy needs some

FOOD.

Once he sleeps or eats his lunch

he's in a

better mood.

Charlie tries to find new ways to share what's on his mind.

His mommies love him even when his ACTIONS are not KIND.

Charlie feels better when he doesn't **hit** and **scream.**

And both his mommies like it when he **isn't being mean.**

Charlie says he's
SORRY
as he's tucked in bed so snug.

Mommy says,
"I forgive you,"
and gives him a
GIANT HUG.

About the Authors

Joy Hoffman is a Korean American transracial adoptee and mother of two biracial children, one of whom is autistic. Joy worked in higher education for twenty-four years before transitioning to independent consulting.

Danielle Kleist is a Korean American transracial adoptee and mother of two biracial children. Danielle worked in higher education for over ten years before transitioning to consulting with Proof Leadership and being a stay-at-home mom.

Danielle & Joy met in 2009 and found a deep connection through their adoptee experiences. They have had a sisterhood ever since and often joke about being twins separated at birth (despite a twenty-year age difference). This book series is a labor of sisterly love.

Follow us on Facebook!
Seoul Sisters Books

About the Illustrator

Matthew E. Howard has been surprising his two daughters with drawings in their lunch boxes since they started school. They are teenagers and still enjoy sketches from their beloved stay-at-home dad. Matt enjoys golfing, exercising, cooking, and family time. He is also a biracial American and Army veteran with a background in marketing & sales. This is his first children's book, which he is illustrating with his sister, Danielle.